# 3 O'CLOCK
## IN THE MORNING

by

Beryl Kemp

# 3 O' CLOCK IN THE MORNING

# 3 O'CLOCK
## IN THE MORNING

by

Beryl Kemp

# 3 O'CLOCK IN THE MORNING

Copyright 2009

by Beryl Kemp

All Rights reserved

Unless otherwise noted, Scripture quotations taken from the HOLY BIBLE,
NEW INTERNATIONAL VERSION.
Copyright (c) 1973, 1978, 1984 by International Bible Society.
Used by permission of Hodder & Stoughton, a member of the
Hodder Headline Group.

Published by: Concord Designs (U.K.)
Printed in Malaysia by Cosmic Master Printing Sdn. Bhd
No. 6, Jalan Permas 12/14, Bandar Baru Permas Jaya,
81750 Masai, Johor Darul Ta'zim, West Malaysia.
Tel: 607-3863493   Fax: 607-3863495
Email: cosmicprint@yahoo.com

ISBN 978-0-9563309

This 'little' book

is dedicated to my husband Keith

for all his love, patience, understanding

and for not complaining when the light is on at

3 o'clock in the morning.

…………

This little book is not intended to advise you on

## How To Get Back To Sleep

But rather thoughts on

## How To Use The Time While You Are Awake.

This is a 'Little' book on purpose

it has been designed this way.

WHY ?

I will tell you why.

Because at 3 o'clock in the morning who wants to

open a big book, hold a big book and read a big book?

This 'Little' book is meant to help solve problems,

not be one.

## Chapter 1

Dear reader, what is it about 3 o'clock in the morning?

Why does it always seem to be in the middle of the night when we wake up?

Why is it the first thing most of us do is start immediately worrying and fretting about our problems, our health, our loved ones?

How can we change ourselves, our family, perhaps even our friends, or our circumstances?

Our illnesses become critical, our debts become insurmountable. What he said and she said and they said becomes almost unbearable. Sick and in pain, wounded in body and spirit, everything seemingly impossible; the mountain too high the valley too wide.

Could this be you right now?

Well, I am here to tell you that you are not alone.

Now, that has to be the best news you could wish to hear at this moment in your life. I believe that there is a God and His name is Jesus and if you will allow me the privilege of becoming your friend I would like to introduce you to Him and since we are getting to know each other my name is Beryl and I think I shall just call you Reader from now on if that's all right with you?

So here goes, from here on in it is just between the three of us Jesus, Reader and Beryl.

Sounds good to me; hope it does to you...........................

I think I should start by telling you a little about myself. You will have gathered that I am a Christian and can't even begin to imagine my life without Jesus and His word the Bible. I am also a wife and mother, sister, mother-in-law and grandma and everything else that goes along with all those titles, (taxi driver, cook and general 'gofer' comes to mind). I must admit though that I do draw the line at washing dishes and have the luxury of a dishwasher affectionately called Ethel. I work full time in Sales and all in all I am a pretty busy lady. So why am I writing this 'little' book for you?

Well, since becoming a Christian I just wanted to know more and more about Him. His work, His ministry, the Old Testament, the New Testament just everything I could lay my hands on, but where to find the time? I guess I didn't realise it at first but gradually it dawned on me that I was waking up at around 3 o'clock morning after morning. I was wide awake and so all the usual 'thoughts and worries' would start filling my mind but I was a Christian, wasn't I? Well yes! So as the saying goes "What would Jesus do?" I had to find out.

I began putting my bedside light on and opening my Bible and doing just that, finding out. The answers are all in there dear Reader, all in there. As I read the words, suddenly, it became not just a book but it was as if God Himself was speaking to me, just for me. The words I read spoke directly into my situation, my mind and my heart. The Bible is all about ordinary people doing extraordinary things for God and through God. It was amazing and still is.

Well I am ordinary; so why God are you waking me up at 3 o'clock?

I began keeping a little book. Not a diary and not every night but just when I really felt under pressure, or anxious, weary or even sad. My private 'little book' of thoughts took me about 5 years to fill. Page after page of just ordinary happenings, day by day, ups and downs, mountains and valley experiences, just life and the living of it.

# 3 O' CLOCK IN THE MORNING

Then God spoke to me "Beryl write a book" I heard Him say it into my Spirit and again "Beryl write a book." "But Lord I can't write a book; what can I write about?" For weeks I thought of subjects, fiction, romance, travel. Oh this was just too silly I thought, I must have not heard right, perhaps it was for someone else, yes, I was to watch and see and then I would recognise the person and I should then encourage them to write something amazing for God. Yes! that was the answer, that was it. That night I opened my Bible at random, *Jeremiah Chapter 30*. My eyes went immediately to *verse 2* "This is what the Lord, the God of Israel, says:

*"Write in a book all the words I have spoken to you"* "Oh no! not again Lord ! You have the wrong person. I can't write a book" and the Lord said quite clearly:

*"You already have"*

"All those early mornings when you talked to me and I spoke to you and you wrote them down, those things weren't just for you but they were to share with other ordinary people going through their tough times, their troubled times, their mountain times, their valley times. Their 'times' are also in my hand. Tell them what I told you."

I hope and pray that this 'little' book will help you even if it just says, someone else understands, someone else cares. When all seems lost and the sky is dark and there seems no end to it all. God cares, He loves you, He is speaking to you. He speaks to ordinary people in extraordinary ways. He speaks in love and with wisdom. His time is not our time, sometime we wonder when He is coming, but believe me, He is never late.

Read and rest, Read and rest.

God Bless You and Keep You
Love Beryl

## Chapter 2

I don't know about you Reader but I am feeling more and more that we are getting to know each other so let's move on and share some time and thoughts together. I feel that we should first ask Jesus to pray with us before we venture any further. The Bible does say in *Matthew 18:20*

*Where two or more are gathered together in His name He will be with us.*

Maybe you once knew Jesus and have drifted away, maybe you have never met him so perhaps now is the time. Whatever the past holds the fact remains that you are awake reading this little book so the three of us are in this together.

### Prayer time.

*Dear Lord Jesus,*

*I really am a little nervous talking to you on a one to one basis never having done it before. I do feel now is a good time to get to know you, please. I am told that in the book of Matthew Chapter 7 verses 7-9 it tells me to Ask, Seek and Knock. Well, I am certainly asking. As for seeking... not a word I've ever used much except I remember as a child playing Hide and Seek. If the person hiding was in a good place, it used to take ages to find them so I guess I have been looking, sorry, seeking for you for quite some time and looking in all the wrong places but I really do want to find you and know you now. If you're real, then, be real to me. I'm tired of being in all the wrong places. Sometimes I don't feel worth anything at all, but I do know that you died for me on a cross but quite honestly, I don't understand fully why you did that. It must have been so cruel and unimaginably awful but you did all that suffering so that I wouldn't have to. I feel so burdened with one thing and another that's going on in my life. Can I share my problems with you, please? I lay it on the line Jesus I am a sinner! You know, suddenly I'm beginning to sense that I am walking in a place I've never been before; just talking to you started out being so hard but somehow now I've got going it's all getting, well, easier. I just know that you love me, just as I am.*

*Repentance, I've never used that word before either. If it means I'm sorry then, well, I repent. I'm going to turn around and leave my past behind me now that I know I have you in my life as my Saviour, My Lord and my Friend. There's a long road stretching out ahead of me but I've got a fresh start. Does this mean I've been born again it certainly feels like it.*

*Thank you Jesus, thank you so much. Amen.*

Hi Reader, its me again. I am so glad you said all that to Jesus. I just know that the three of us are going to have a great time together. What I've done is put some of my own 3 o'clock-in-the-morning times down on paper for us to look at together. I've written them roughly in A-Z order but of course I didn't experience them that way, but thought it would be an easy way of doing it. Remember this is also 'a first' for me so you're not the only one learning new things.

Now buy yourself a good NIV Bible (or whichever version you prefer.) from a Christian bookshop. Get a note pad and pen, a small bedside lamp and let's begin the journey.

I have put some blank pages at the end of the book, if you prefer you can use those, that way what you write won't get lost and you might even start your own 'little' book.

## Psalm 121

*I will lift up my eyes to the hills  - where does my help come from?*
*My help comes from the Lord, the Maker of heaven and earth.*

*He will not let your foot slip – he who watches over you will not slumber; indeed, he who watches over Israel will neither slumber nor sleep.*

*The Lord watches over you – the Lord  is your shade at your right hand; the sun shall not harm you by day,*
  *nor the moon by night.*

  *The Lord will keep you from all harm – he will watch over your life; the Lord will watch over your coming and going both now and evermore.*

Now this seems to be saying to me. Get your head up and stop looking down at your boots and all your problems. God wants to help you. He is bigger than you and after all he did make all the earth and the heavens, no small achievement would you say. He is not going to let you fall, he is watching you 24/7. Nothing will harm (hurt) you as long as you stay close. He will not move away, you have to do the moving !!!

This is only the Beryl version and you understand that I am just like you 'ordinary' but I know how awesome He is.

## 3 O' CLOCK IN THE MORNING

I know it's late Reader

(or rather it's early!)

so to try to make things easier

I've made a list of headings

over the page

and hope that one

fits the struggle

you may be facing tonight.

~

# Contents

# 3 O' CLOCK IN THE MORNING

## Anxious Thoughts

Are you awake Reader? I am.

Is everywhere quiet? I mean it is 3 o'clock isn't it!

Perhaps you can hear the sound of it raining outside, gentle drizzle or is it throwing it down? Maybe the wind is howling or just maybe, just maybe it is just still, no noise, peaceful and quiet. No children's voices, no one 'needing' you. No one wanting you 'to do' something for them, no phone ringing, no TV blaring away.....just quiet. Just you awake listening to your own anxious thoughts.

Well I am here to tell you that whatever you may be thinking you are definitely not on your own. OK you feel lonely but you are not on your own. In **Matthew 28: v 20** Jesus says.

*"And surely I am with you always, to the very end of the age"*

Now that sounds like a promise to me so rather than go round and round in your head about things that quite honestly you can't do anything about right now, (lets face facts you are in bed aren't you!) Talk about what's making you anxious and troubling you through with Him.

*Psalm 121* clearly tells us that He is awake too and 'No' you needn't try to be clever or hide anything (actually He knows it already but he wants to hear it from you) so tell it like how it is. Here is something I have learnt if it will help. I have found that when I am talking it is so much harder to listen at the same time so whatever the devil is trying to get you to believe in one ear you can't hear because your mouth is … get the picture. Here are some verses you could start looking up.

*Joshua 1: 9 - "Have I not commanded you? Be strong and of good courage; do not be afraid, nor be dismayed, for the LORD your God is with you wherever you go."*

*Proverbs 16:3 - "Commit your works to the LORD, And your thoughts will be established."*

*Proverbs 3:5-6 - "Trust in the LORD with all your heart, And lean not on your own understanding; In all your ways acknowledge Him, And He shall direct your paths."*

*Luke 11:9 - "So I say to you, ask and it will be given to you; seek, and you will find; knock, and it will be opened to you."*

Try to get some sleep now,
Love you,
Beryl.

## Blessings

I will start you off: I was blessed today because........

I was warm and had enough to eat. A friend rang me and offered to give me a lift, which I really appreciated. I found a little white fluffy feather just by my car door and it was as if it had been placed there just for me. It was so pretty. Most importantly of all, I am blessed because Jesus loves me and whether I have a little or a lot I have learned to be happy. His grace and mercy are new every morning.

Every day we all receive a full 24 hours, rich or poor we all get the same. The Bible tells us that we are blessed so that we can be a blessing. Try it tomorrow, being a blessing to someone else. You make someone happy. Oh, I know you don't feel like it right now but go on, just give it a try.

Jabez actually *asked* the Lord to bless him.

### *The Jabez Prayer*

*Jabez cried out to the God of Israel,*
*"Oh, that you would bless me*
*and enlarge my territory!*
*Let your hand be with me,*
*and keep me from harm so*
*that I wil be free from pain!"*
*And God granted his request.*

### *1 Chronicles 4:10*

You might want to go and buy the book by Bruce Wilkinson, I thoroughly recommend it. Also while you are in the Christian bookshop buy 'Footprints' it is usually on a little card and you can pop it into your wallet or purse.

True happiness really doesn't depend on our emotions being up or down, that's life and we have to learn to take the rough with the smooth. When we get to know Him, and discovering who we are in Him and that we are truly loved, being at peace on the inside, just then and only then will we begin to get a glimpse of a different kind of happiness.

It's the sort that other people recognise and simply can't explain. A smile that lights up the room, a cheery word when all looks black; a peace, contentment, an unspeakable joy. A fire that no one or no 'thing' can put out.


Good night and God Bless
Sleep well
Love, Beryl

## Comfort

"Are you sitting comfortably? Then, I'll begin" How many times as a child did you hear that and knew you were going to have a story read to you. You sat cross legged and waited eagerly for what was to come. Something nice was about to happen. I hope you are 'comfortable' Reader. Warm bed, comfy pillows, and pleasant room. Well, I am not going to tell you a make-believe bedtime story, sorry. What I have to say isn't all about you being comfortable but about being comforted and giving comfort to others.

The prophet Isaiah said in **Chapter 40 Verse 1**

*"Comfort, comfort my people says your God"* very clear instruction here wouldn't you say? Sounds like he means what he says, repeating himself like that.

Then in *2 Corinthians Chapter 1: 3-7* .

*The God of All Comfort*

*Praise be to the God and Father of our Lord Jesus Christ, the Father of compassion and the God of comfort, who comforts us in our troubles, so that we can comfort those in any trouble with the comfort we ourselves have received from God. For just as the sufferings of Christ flow over our lives, so also through Christ our comfort overflows.*

*If we are distressed, it is for your comfort and salvation; if we are comforted, it is for your comfort, which produces in you patient endurance of the same sufferings we suffer.*

*And our hope for you is firm, because we know that just as you share in our sufferings, so also you share in our comfort.*

Just as Isaiah repeats himself here, so does Paul. All to add emphasis. God comforts you and you are to comfort others. He knows our suffering; he comforts us so that we can learn how to comfort others.

Got the message!

You know, God has a way of dealing with us at our point of need but it shouldn't and mustn't stop there. You have been blessed, now look to others to be a blessing.

*Comfort those who mourn (Isaiah 61:2) give them comfort and joy (Jeremiah 31: 13)*

*encouragement and comfort (1 Cor.14:3) so that through Christ our comfort overflows (2 Cor.1:5)*

I hope that you don't think I am making light of the sadness you may be feeling just now. You need comforting and Jesus in His mercy will supply all your needs.

What the word is telling us is that it shouldn't and mustn't stop there.

*Freely you have received, freely give. Matthew 10 v 8*

Good night and God bless, hope you feel better soon.
Love, Beryl.

## David & Goliath

### (Facing your giants)

The shepherd boy David was the youngest son of Jesse. He looked after the sheep. I guess you have heard the story, maybe as a child, of how he, with a sling and 5 small smooth pebbles killed the big giant.

Well Reader, I want you to read the full account in your Bible. It is only a chapter and won't take you long. You will find it in *1 Samuel Chapter 17.*

Forget the kid's stuff, this was real. There was fear in the camp. Two opposing armies ready for war. The Philistine's had this champion called Goliath. He was a giant of a man standing between 8 and 9ft. tall. (my bedroom, floor to ceiling is about 8ft! just to give you something to visualise) this guy was probably pretty broad as well so I think we might describe him as awesome. (If he said it was Monday, it was Monday!)

This huge giant would come out daily, shouting, challenging someone to fight him. He wore full armour *(v 4-8)* and this in itself must have been a fearsome sight, yes there was definitely fear there in the valley. Yet along comes David, full of faith in his God wondering why everyone is so afraid. In a nutshell David overcame the giant with a single stone and killed him. He even cut off Goliath's head with the giant's own sword.

In another account Moses sent twelve spies into the Promised Land and ten came back with stories of giants (descendants of Anak; as Goliath was) this time it was the Valley of Eshcol. You find this in *Numbers 13* again the whole chapter. Only Caleb and Joshua came back and wanted to go in and claim the land but the others only saw the giants.

*Verse 33*, the last verse seems to say it all.

*"We saw the Nephilim there.* (the descendants of Anak came from Nephilim) *We seemed like grasshoppers in our own eyes, and we looked the same to them."*

When you have a 'giant' to face, - a huge problem, a debt, a meeting with a difficult person perhaps, whatever the giant may be, if you see yourself small the giant will too. What to do? Pray and put on the whole armour of God. "How do I do that?" I can hear you saying it! Well, read *Ephesians 6: v10-18*

*"Finally be strong in the Lord and in His mighty power. Put on the full armour of God so that you can take your stand against the devil's schemes. For our struggle is not against flesh and blood, but against the rulers, against the authorities, against the powers of this dark world and against the spiritual forces of evil in the heavenly realms.*

*Therefore put on the full armour of God, so that when the day of evil comes, you may be able to stand your ground, after you have done everything, to stand. Stand firm then, with the belt of truth buckled round your waist, with the breastplate of righteousness in place, and with your feet fitted with the readiness that comes from the gospel of peace.*

*In addition to all this, take up the shield of faith, with which you can extinguish all the flaming arrows of the evil one. Take the helmet of salvation and the sword of the Spirit on all occasions with all kinds of prayers and requests. With this in mind, be alert and always keep on praying for all the saints.*

With God's armour on, you can face your 'giant', do it in fear and trembling maybe but do it. Very often it turns out to be quite different from what you expected. Please don't be foolhardy but try to understand what I am trying to say. David had killed a lion and a bear while he had been on his own looking after his father's sheep. Now he was ready and able to face the giant. Maybe God has been preparing you when you were in a different time and place in your life. A situation you felt you couldn't cope with but you did it and came through. Maybe a meeting you had dreaded but you went and faced up to the person, could even be that there have been many 'small' incidents that you have come through and so now, maybe you are more prepared than you think. God has been by your side before, could be you just didn't know Him then. But now… you could be more prepared than you could ever imagine.

Good night.
God Bless
Love, Beryl

# Eagles

**Isaiah 40: 29-31**

*He gives strength to the weary*
*And increases the power of the weak.*
*Even youths grow tired and weary,*
*And young men stumble and fall;*
*But those who hope in the Lord*
*Will renew their strength.*
*They will soar on wings like eagles;*
*They will run and not grow weary,*
*They will walk and not be faint.*

My hope is that these verses will encourage and inspire you, dear Reader. I know they always do me. When all of life seems to crowd in around you so you feel you can hardly breathe, visualise the mighty eagle soaring on the thermals high over the mountain peaks.

Let your spirit soar, glide effortlessly, allow the wind to sweep away the cares and be renewed. God understands your weariness and will lift you up. Your hope will rise and you will find the strength once more to run and to walk the allotted course marked out for you. His grace is sufficient.

May God bless you and keep you.

Sleep Well.
Love, Beryl

## Feeling Down

Did you go to bed feeling down? Not depressed, just 'down'. I really do think we are too quick these days to use the word 'depression' when sometimes; just sometimes we are thoroughly fed up with life, ourselves, everybody else, just everything. Bed is the only option at this point. Go to sleep and not get up again. How bad is that?

Depression is such a huge subject so I am not going there with you. Neither this little book nor I am big enough for that. No let's just say you're down in the dumps.

Sometimes, there is a physical problem causing the 'down' feelings. My mum had two reasons and two reasons only if I had a long face. Either I was tired and should get to bed early or I must be 'run down' because I needed more sleep (too many late nights) I was whisked off to the doctor's for a 'tonic' (usually something full of iron) or at the worst I was persuaded that cooked liver would make a new woman of me. Ugh! Sorry, you might like it.

Very often the cause can be traced back to the fact that someone has said something to hurt or upset you and all you've done since is keep mulling it over, regurgitate it and gone into the 'if only' debate with yourself. Usually it's not what you said but what you didn't say that really irritates you but for now you are hurt and deflated like a big balloon that has been burst. They've ruined your day and you are carrying it into the night, in fact you've woken up and it's the first thing on your mind. Ask yourself, "Is it really worth it?"

Please don't think though that I am making light of your feelings. Worry, hopelessness or feeling worthless. I so hope that's not you tonight, dear Reader. I have no way of telling why you feel this way right now. Money worries and the panic of unpaid bills (we will deal with this in 'Money' later). Fed up with scrimping and scraping, making ends meet. Finally you feel you can't take any more. You are literally worn out both in mind and body.

*"Lord help us to light the fire of hope. Kindle a flame that will burn away all the dross in our lives and enable us to see what is really important and help us to make a way where there seems to be no way." Amen*

*Psalm 42 verses 5 and 11* (but read the whole *Psalm*)

*Why are you downcast, O my soul?*

*Why so disturbed within me?*

*Put your hope in God for I will yet praise him*

*My Saviour and my God.*

Remember 'there's a new day coming' so try to sleep

Good night
God Bless
Love, Beryl

## Going Through

*Philippians Chapter 4 v 13*

*I can do everything through Him who gives me strength.*

Hello, Reader. How are you? Are you by any chance going 'through' something in your life right now? Could it be that you are awake reading because of the troubles you are going through?

*David says in Psalm 23:*

*Yea though I walk through the valley of the shadow of death I will fear no evil.*

There are always things we have to go through, everybody does. Exams, tests and temptations - they are all part of life's rich tapestry. I got through my GCSE's, I managed to get through my driving test, I got through a whole week without a cigarette, a drink or what ever. For me it was biting my nails. No big deal some say but for me it was very difficult. You go through tunnels, through the woods, through the valley, usually all long dark shadowy places. Funny but no one ever talks about going through happy, amazing times in our lives but if they do you find they add something to the 'through' that changes it completely. I sailed through, I battled through or I fought my way through. Notice the adjectives used they are 'fighting talk', strength is required and where do we find our strength? Yes that's it, say it out loud.

*I can do everything through Him who gives me strength.*

Copy out this verse and stick it onto the fridge, onto your mirror, in your car, everywhere and anywhere where you will see it all the time. Remember it, say it, do it. Go through and learn on the way.

"I went through hell and high water,"
"I went through so many sleepless nights"
"I'm not going through that anymore."

You see all these things we say, you're either going through negative or positive. Forging through or crying all the way, there is a choice. Oh and as my Pastor Clive Corfield says, " Don't pitch your tent in the valley, keep on going through." I repeat this in 'Valleys' but it is so important that we do get the message, keep on keeping on.

***Jesus equips us for the battle you know, yes, He does! and He gives us the armour for the fight too!***

***Ephesians Chapter 6 verses 10 – 18*** (by the way you will find this on the page where we deal with Giants)

Go to sleep now.
God Bless.
Love, Beryl

## Happy

You've turned to the page headed Happy. Is it because you are happy tonight, Reader? I do hope so but maybe it's because you're just the opposite. I have no way of telling but rest assured He knows. So let's all talk about it together. I mean what's all this H. A. P. P. Y. stuff about anyway! Don't get me wrong if you are awake because you are happy then that is just great and I am so pleased for you. However, if it is because you are not, then that's a different matter.

What makes a person feel happy? I think I will use the word 'Happenings', things that happen to us make us happy or sad. Sometimes, it just depends on the way we look at a situation. You know the, "Is the glass half full or half empty" thing. Think about it for a minute. Or, perhaps, were you relying on some people today to make you happy and they've let you down? Just maybe they don't even realise it. They are probably fast asleep. Don't get mad – get over it. OK, they have hurt you, but humans do this all the time, sometimes on purpose granted, but just sometimes they really are quite unaware of what they have done. Would discussing it help or just cause an argument? Pray about this one, it could be tricky.

There is also the possibility, dear Reader that you are unhappy because you simply didn't get your own way. I know, I know that's a hard one to take but that's what friends are for and after all there is only you at this pity party and you're not having such a good time are you?

Why not think about what you have got, rather than think about what you have not! Like blessings, for instance.

Just a thought to sleep on maybe!

(Perhaps you could make a list on one of those blank pages, after all that's what they are there for)

## Illness or Healing

Hello, Reader, I wonder what's brought you to this chapter tonight? Are things not right with you? Are you ill or has someone close to you had bad news, is the diagnosis what you had been dreading certainly not what you wanted to hear? So many raw emotions, fear, panic, tears, Oh! so many tears! Questions, so many questions, "Why, God Why?"

"Why me God?" "Why my family?" There are murderers walking the street in complete health, "Why?" "God, Why Me?"

And silence is all you hear.

I wish there was an easy answer. Oh! how I wish I could tell you the answer to your question, but I can't. You see there just isn't an answer. There isn't an easy explanation as to why people suffer. How often have we heard the question and heard only silence. Sometimes, we try to do everything 'right', or at least what we think or what the books say, is right and still the inevitable happens. Sometimes, we get ill and it is partly our own fault. We do things to excess and our bodies simply can't cope. My own mum never drank or smoked; she worked hard, loved us and all her family dearly. She helped people all she could, did good deeds daily and died a painful death with cancer. God didn't heal her body although we pleaded and prayed. He could have done but what he did do was even more amazing. I watched as her body diminished to a shadow and her bones wither away but she found a new strength and a courage that was evident to everyone around her the nearer and nearer she came to meet with God. Her faith grew and grew and she went to heaven praising Him her Saviour and her King. Her courage came the day she read *Psalm 139*. "He knows me" she greeted me with one day as I walked into the Hospice. "He knows me inside and out."

The thing is He knows you too. He is here with you tonight. Share your anxious thoughts and fears with him. The shortest sentence in the Bible is in *John 11 v 35* I think you should read the whole chapter but for now the sentence is

*'Jesus wept'*

He knows what you are going through, He feels your pain, He loves you.

Try to sleep now
God Bless you,
Love, Beryl

# Journeys

Reader just do yourself a favour, get a pen and paper and make a list. You are going away and don't want to forget anything so make a list. Just do it. You have a lot on your mind, you mustn't forget anything so write it down.

Toothpaste, tickets, book, keys.

Is it a holiday you're looking forward to or a journey you would rather not be taking? Perhaps your list has toothpaste, letter, book, dressing gown. Is a hospital bed waiting for you rather than a hotel bedroom?

*Matthew 11 v 28*

*"Come to me, all you who are weary and burdened, and I will give you rest."*

Our lives are a series of journeys. Unknown places, unknown destinations. For some it's darkest Africa, for few it's the moon and for many simply going from room to room. Big steps, little steps still a journey. I am aware it is 3 in the morning, my dear Reader but I have the desire to take you on an unexpected journey. Please will you come? You will? Great.

Pack a bag.

Here is a new list of things to put in it and maybe you can add some more:

Worries, anxieties, troubles, hurts, pain, grief, lies, fear, debt, selfishness, pride, sin.

There is still room, pack everything in; it's a big bag. Now pick up your bag. I know it's heavy but you've been carrying all those things round for a long time. It's just they are all in one bag now. Look up, there is a hill in front of you, start walking, it's a bit of a climb but get going. This time you're on your own for a bit but I will talk you through.

Keep going, now ahead of you what can you see on the horizon? Yes, that's right. It is a cross. Draw closer, yes there is a man, he is hanging on the cross. You are cold Reader but keep looking, keep going. Nearer and nearer. You are there, at the foot of the cross.

Put your bag down Reader and look up. Yes his feet. Oh look! There, thick rough nails hammered through his feet, there's so much blood and dirt but keep looking Reader, so much blood, so much pain. He has been beaten, whipped, bruised, his hands are stretched out and more nails, more blood spilt, poured out. His head, can you bear to look into his face, his poor face almost unrecognisable, thick thorns piercing into his forehead, blood, tears mingled together. It is unbearable to look but wait, he is saying something.

**_"Father, forgive them, for they do not know what they are doing"_**

**_Luke 23 v 34_**

Oh my Lord what have I done to you? Oh my Lord, what have you done for me!

Accept his love, dear Reader, leave your bag where it is. Ask for forgiveness. He has dealt with it all. It is His free gift.
You had to make the journey.


I am crying dear friend, maybe you are crying, too. You are in bed but how far you have come. Still one more thing. Go stand behind the cross. Feel the love, the warmth, hear the sound of praise of singing. Look around you, see the thousands upon thousands of souls worshipping God their Saviour and yours. You are in the kingdom, you're forgiven. A new journey has just begun. Pack a new bag, fill it this time with love, mercy, forgiveness, hope, joy, peace and so much more.

There's a new day dawning, enjoy the journey. Sleep well, Jesus loves you.

## Keep Watching for Opportunities

Hello Reader, how are you tonight? You know I'm lying here just thinking, how many opportunities have I missed in my life? Have you ever wondered that? It really is hard to tell, isn't it? The 'Big' obvious ones that stared us right in the face and we pondered on and then let go are now just memories, but what about the ones we missed? We just didn't recognise what they were until perhaps it was too late.

*Galatians 6 v 10:*

***Therefore, as we have opportunity, let us do good to all people, especially to those who belong to the family of believers.***

Opportunities therefore aren't always chances to do something for ourselves. God puts circumstances in our path whereby we can do something for someone else and often end up being blessed ourselves. Don't hold back therefore when you see a need or a chance to do something, however small for someone else. Sometimes there could be an opportunity to change direction in life, a new job, travel or move house. We may choose to let the opportunity pass but then that is a decision we have to live with, hence the need to pray and seek God's direction. Daily we make decisions. Daily opportunities occur to simply tell someone we love them. Don't put off the picnic with the kids, or the meal with a friend, take the flowers, write the card, make the phone call.

*Colossians 4 v 5 & 6* (I always have trouble finding Colossians. Do you? It's after Philippians and only has 4 chapters)

***Be wise in the way you act towards outsiders; make the most of every opportunity.***

Sadly in life there are others who also watch for opportunities. Often with the intent to harm or disgrace us. Look what happened to Jesus.

*Mark 14 v10 & 11*

*Then Judas Iscariot, one of the Twelve, went to the chief priests to betray Jesus to them.*

*They were delighted to hear this and promised to give him money. So he watched for an opportunity to hand him over.*

Have you felt the injustice of being 'handed over' simply because others were jealous or greedy?

I urge you to take it to the Lord in prayer; there is nothing he doesn't understand. Allow him to deal with it. Maybe you feel like you are in the Garden of Gethsemane tonight. He's been there, he knows. Resolve to move forward, reach out to others. Be salt and light in this dull world.

*Romans 12 v 2*

*Do not conform any longer to the pattern of this world, but be transformed by the renewing of your mind. Then you will be able to test and approve what God's will is - his good, pleasing and perfect will.*

God will set before you more opportunities, recognise them as such. Be blessed.

Good night dear friend.
God bless
Love, Beryl

## Level

*Isaiah 40: v 4:*

*Every valley shall be raised up,*
*Every mountain and hill made low;*
*The rough ground shall become level,*
*The rugged places plain.*
*And the glory of the Lord will be revealed,*
*And all mankind together will see it.*
*For the mouth of the Lord has spoken.*

Has it been all ups and downs lately dear Reader? Feeling a bit like a yo-yo with someone else pulling the string? Life is like that, sometimes. Mountains rising up as if from nowhere, valleys opening wide swallowing you.

You are lying in bed now wondering what new obstacle you will find in your path tomorrow. The verse from Isaiah tells us that God will go before us and level everything out for us. Again and again we are urged to put our trust in Him and He will make our paths smooth and level.

*Proverbs 4 v 10-12:*

*Listen, my son, accept what I say,*
*And the years of your life will be many.*
*I guide you in the way of wisdom and lead you along straight paths.*
*When you walk, your steps will not be hampered;*
*When you run, you will not stumble.*

" Lord I pray with my friend Reader right now as we share these thoughts together, that you will hear our prayer and guide us in the ways that we should go. That you will go before us and make level paths for our feet, that we should not stumble and fall but walk with boldness knowing that you are with us.

Thank you Lord for Your loving kindness, Your grace and mercy.

Amen and amen."

Mountains and valleys can be beautiful places, too, you know. Don't always see them as obstacles. Mountains that have been climbed have been conquered and the view from up there can be amazing. Valleys can be peaceful and lush with sweeping shadows as a cloud crosses the sun and creates a strange beauty. Life is not all about stumbling over rocks when God is holding your hand and leading, so go on let Him lead. Maybe you have been let down by someone in the past and now fear being led?

God is not a man that he should lie; He loves you; He won't let you fall. As you submit yourself to Him you will find yourself becoming stronger, more confident, more able to discern the people around you. Really, this is true. Wherever you are or whatever you are doing, keep saying "Lord, am I on the right track, am I going the right way, is this the way I should be going?" When you keep asking others sometime they all come up with a different answer and you could end up more confused than ever.

. Ask God first.

I will leave you with *Psalm 143: v10*

*Teach me to do your will,*
*For you are my God;*
*May your good Spirit lead me on level ground.*


Good night and God Bless dear friend.
Sleep well.

## Money

What shall we say about money!

If you were to stop someone in the street and say to them, "What does the Bible say about money?" in all probability they would most likely reply,

"Money is the root of all evil" when actually what the Bible says, and you can find it for yourself in *1 Timothy 6 v10:*

*"For the love of money is a root of all kinds of evil. Some people, eager for money, have wandered from the faith and pierced themselves with many griefs."*

Note the love of money, not money itself, quite different don't you think? Actually the Bible has a great deal to say about money starting in *Genesis 17: v 12* right through to *1 Peter 5: 2*. There are lots of debates, even arguments we could get into Reader but it is 3 o'clock in the morning and if you are worried over money, and I am presuming, the lack of it and debt is knocking at your door, then I also know that you are in no mood for debate.

You are more likely than not gripped with nerve-racking panic wondering just where the next penny is going to come from when you get up in the morning. Let's be honest most of us have been caught up in the 'buy now pay later' trap. It all looked so easy, have the goods now and pay in two, three or five years down the road. You convinced yourself it was for the best. We'll be better off then, the promotion will have come, the kids will have grown and gone, the car will be paid for. But it hasn't and debt has piled on top of debt. Something else cropped up in the middle somewhere out of the blue and now... well now there just isn't enough to juggle with anymore and fear and worry consume you and there seems just no way out.

A great deep pit and nothing to hang on to. If it's any consolation Reader, you're not on your own it's just that we can't talk about it, it hurts too much, it is just too awful. Thousands are caught like frightened rabbits in the car headlights. From the poor man in the street to the 'rich' man in his castle, money worries grip and gnaw at his soul.

*Ecclesiastes Ch. 5: 10*

*"Whoever loves money never has money enough; whoever loves wealth is never satisfied with his income. This too is meaningless."*

Sadly we can't live without money but we are to be wise, the man who spends more than he earns is looking at a bleak future.

*Matthew Ch 6: v 24*

*"No one can serve two masters. Either he will hate the one and love the other, or he will be devoted to the one and despise the other. You cannot serve God and Money."*

I love this verse from the prophet *Isaiah Ch 52: v 3*
For this is what the Lord says:

*"You were sold for nothing, and without money you will be redeemed"*

The Lord says He will provide for all our needs (note not our 'wants').
God knows all about money it isn't a subject we mustn't mention. The Bible is full of references to money, look them all up, it will amaze you. You give back to God and He will provide for you. God doesn't 'need' your money; what He desires is your obedience. Your reverential love and obedience. He loves you so much He doesn't want you in debt to anyone except Him through His death

on the cross and He did that willingly out of love for you. Our tithes and offerings are His, He gave them to us.

*Malachi Ch 3: v 6* onwards is headed 'Robbing God'. A strange thing to say you might think but carefully read what it says.

*Verse 10: "Bring the whole tithe into the storehouse* (that's 10% of your earnings to the place where you are 'fed', your local church, or maybe a ministry that you watch on TV) *that there may be food in my house. Test me in this, says the Lord Almighty, And see if I will not throw open the floodgates of heaven and pour out so much blessing that you will not have room for it."*

Do read the whole chapter Reader. Granted it is a hard one to do but the Lord does make a promise and He is not a man to lie. We are blessed to become a blessing. I urge you to think deeply about your 'coming in's and your going out's. You are to be a good steward with the little you have and God will see and bless you. Why would He give you more money if you don't do what is right with a little?

It is hard I know and I don't have all the answers but I do know that God will provide.

Finally read *Isaiah Chapter 55*. It will inspire and encourage you, pray to God and He will give you comfort and rest from all your anxious thoughts.

Good night and God bless.
Love, Beryl

## Nothing Going Right

Hi there, Reader, you awake again? Me, too!

Are you going through one of those 'seasons' in your life when just everything you touch seems to go wrong; in fact nothing seems to be going right at the moment. If I say it's black, someone argues it's white. I'm not awkward, am I? Is it me?

Well, I know you might wonder if I really do understand how you feel, but I do, I really do. Let me reassure you that we all have these 'patches' when nothing at all is plain sailing so if I make a suggestion will you at least think about it? (please!)

What I am going to suggest is that you take a step back from the situation at the moment, draw an imaginary line and say to yourself, "This is it, this is where it stops, and from now on I'm going to trust in God my Saviour. I am going to put my faith in Him. He knows me better than anyone, he only wants the best for me and most of all He loves me."

Look around you, alright, nothing seems to be working out as you thought it was going to but if God knows and He is in control and you are here, then take another look. Maybe there is a work for you to do here or maybe there is a work to be done in you, here just where you are at. Does that make sense? I do hope so.

If you can't be happy in the desert, you'll never be happy in the Promised Land. God took the children of Israel out of Egypt but as the saying goes 'He had to take Egypt out of the children.' By this I mean the old ways, the things they were used to. The years of wandering in the desert, which by the way geographically should have only taken them eleven days actually took them forty years. Therefore try not to be impatient when circumstances don't move as fast as you would like them to. Maybe God has something better waiting for you, or he could be trying to teach you something by experiencing it. Just be open to His guiding, walk by faith and most of all enjoy the journey.

Good night now dear Reader. Pray and ask God by His Holy Spirit to lead and guide you in the way that you should go.

***Matthew 7 verses 13 and 14***

***"Enter through the narrow gate. For wide is the gate and broad is the road that leads to destruction, and many enter through it. But small is the gate and narrow the road that leads to life, and only a few find it."***

God Bless,
Love, Beryl

## On My Own

Did you spot this heading and think that's me; I'm on my own!

Do they really know what it feels like? No one can know how I feel, how can anyone know!' Well, Jesus knows. How do I know? Well take a look at what the Bible says in **Matthew Chapter 26 verses 36- 46** where Jesus is in Gethsemane the night before He was arrested. He asks Peter, James and John his closest disciples, to stay and pray for Him while He goes to pray on His own telling them,

*"My soul is overwhelmed with sorrow to the point of death. Stay here and keep watch with me."*

Not too much to ask  wouldn't you say after all they said He meant to them. He returns later to find them asleep. Some friends! I hear you say. Imagine how Jesus felt.

*"Could you men not keep watch with me for one hour?"* he asked Peter *(verse 40)*

He goes a second and a third time and still they keep falling asleep. How alone He must have felt. He does know, He does care and what's more remember **Psalm 121** at the front of this little book and *verse 4:*

*"Indeed, he who watches over Israel will neither slumber nor sleep."*

That night in the garden of Gethsemane, let's face it, the man sweated blood. Now that's pressure. We think we have stress! He knew what he was going to face the next day and He asked His disciples to stay awake while He prayed and what did they do…. they fell asleep. These were His friends whom He had been so close to for three years. They had eaten, slept and done everything together. They looked to Him for everything and when He needed them, they went to sleep. He had people with him yet He was alone.

He faced up to everything that night, He sought His Father. He prayed, He cried out, He sweated blood and He found what He needed. Notice that the next day when it was all happening He was able to keep quiet and He suffered beyond anything we can ever imagine. Why? Because He loves us and cares for us. He died and went to hell and came back so we wouldn't have to. That's what real love is.

How can you ever imagine that you are on your own? The Bible tells us that now He is seated at the right hand of God ever interceding for us (praying for you and me).

There could be many reasons why you are on your own, dear Reader. Maybe you've chosen to be on your own. Maybe you feel on your own but you are actually living with someone. Death, divorce, break-ups, falling out of love, all end with people being on their own. Some cope, some hate it but there it is and life goes on. You may have 'family' but don't connect with them, funny how often this happens. Shopping for one seems pointless, going out for a meal hardly seems an option, holidays, not easy to contemplate.

Hello Reader, the whole point of this *'little'* book is to let you know that someone cares. Jesus cares. I care. When you stop and think there are an awful lot of folk on their own. Ever think about 'joining' something. I know you don't want to but maybe just maybe you would actually find you enjoyed it and realised everybody else had in fact joined in 'on their own', too. A good church, a night school class, something 'sporty,' dancing, I don't know but whatever you fancy just do it.

"But I'm afraid", well, do it anyway. You'll meet people, make friends. Someone told me that the best vitamin to make friends is B1. (Sorry but I couldn't resist).

Ask Jesus about Angels.

Yes Angels!

Many times in the Bible angels are mentioned. There are all different kinds you know. Yes, really look them up you will be amazed.

**Hebrews 1:14**

**Are not all angels ministering spirits sent to serve those who will inherit salvation.**

Ask Him to send an angel with you when you 'step out in faith'. Remember you may 'feel' lonely but you are never alone.

**Matthew 28:20**

**Surely I am with you always, to the very end of the age.**

Sounds good to me.

Good night and God bless.

## Perseverance

Perhaps God has been telling you to do something and you really believe and want to do it and you have been trying and doing your best but nothing seems to be happening.

Is that where you are at the moment perhaps?

It is so frustrating I know, are you wilting, feel like giving up, thinking just maybe you heard wrong, it's all been a mistake. You are loosing confidence because things aren't happening fast enough. Are you lying in bed thinking it is all a waste of time? Are you pondering on giving up on your dreams?

"How long Lord, do you want me to keep on doing this?" and He comes back to you with just one word.

"Persevere."

"But it is so hard".

"Well who promised you it would be easy?"

"But I can't see anything happening"

"You are just at the seed sowing stage, be patient."

"You don't see what is going on in the dark soil but in due time a tiny shoot appears"

Babies take 9 months, elephants approximately 22 months, different times but both well worth the wait. It is good to look forward. Some people just don't have the patience to wait. We live in a day and an age where everyone wants everything now! Sort of like an instant microwave society.

Perseverance, keep on keeping on.

*Romans Chapter 5: 3- 6*

*Not only so, but we also rejoice in our sufferings, because we know that suffering produces perseverance; perseverance, character; and character hope. And hope does not disappoint us, because God has poured out his love into our hearts by the Holy Spirit, whom he has given us.*

Then again in *James 1: 4* we read:

*Perseverance must finish its work so that you may be mature and complete, not lacking anything.*

Please do remember to read the verses before and after of the scriptures I am pointing you towards so that you may benefit from the fullness of the teaching.

Do you keep starting things and never finishing them simply getting fed up somewhere in the middle? You know there is such a sense of satisfaction and completeness in actually finishing a task and finishing it well. I urge you to try it some time; you may surprise yourself and those around you.

Finally *Hebrews 12: 1*

*Therefore, since we are surrounded by such a great cloud of witnesses, let us throw off everything that hinders or entangles, and let us run the race marked out for us.*

Life is like a race and whether we walk it or run that is not the point but let us do it and finish well. Some of us don't get off to a good start maybe but we do have a hand in how we finish.

Sleep well dear Reader. Good night and God bless.
Love and kisses.

## Quiet

The dictionary says that quiet means silent not noisy, still not moving; gentle, not boisterous, calm placid uneventful, undisturbed peace.

*Psalm 23 v 2*

*He makes me lie down in green pastures,*
*He leads me beside quiet waters he restores my soul.*

Note that He makes me lie down! This Jesus I am introducing you to dear Reader sometimes has to make us lie down. Sometimes, we just don't know when we have done enough or had enough, do we! We go on and on till we drop. Could that be you tonight my dear friend? You have done so much that now you simply are over tired and you just can't sleep however hard you try, the brain is going; you are changing the world and writing notes for tomorrow.

"If I don't do it, no one else will." How many times have I said or heard that one! Take time to go and lay down beside those quiet waters so that he can restore your soul, your soul being your mind, body and spirit. Take care or God may well make you and there will be no choice. Sometimes, you may just need to be quiet, even just going to another room away from all the chatter and television can be enough. We seem to feel we have to be busy all the time these days and that there is something wrong with us if we can't say all the time "Oh, I am so busy, I can hardly breathe." I have also discovered that there are other 'Quiets' we might consider.

*Isaiah 42:14* says

*"For a long time I kept silent I have been quiet and held myself back."*

The next verse begins

*But now…………..*

*Then Isaiah 62:1*

*"For Zion's sake I will not keep silent for Jerusalem's sake I will not remain quiet till righteousness shines out like the dawn".*

Holding back or speaking out, there is a time for both. Jesus himself in **Mark 1:25** doesn't leave the evil spirit in any doubt.

*"Be quiet!"* said Jesus sternly *"come out of him"*

Here quiet is a word of command, no discussion, no option simply

*"Be quiet"*

Some people love being quiet, others hate it. Noise, hustle and bustle are part of daily life but now, right now at 3 o'clock in the morning is it quiet for you, are you enjoying the quiet or is the silence a source of fear? Perhaps you are worrying tonight, dear Reader. The question in your head is "shall you speak up or shall you remain quiet?" Shall you rest in quietness or break free and begin to make yourself heard.
Choices, decisions, maybe this will help.

*Matthew 10:v 27*

*"What I tell you in the dark, speak in the daylight: what is whispered in your ear, proclaim from the roofs."*

Obviously really pray about this and feel really sure, use this 'quiet time' to speak to Jesus and then just be quiet and listen.

Sleep well dear Reader.

God bless.

## Rest

We all need to rest. How about you right now, dear Reader? Have you had some sleep but now it is 3 o'clock in the morning and you find yourself wide awake but weary?

Weary is a funny word not used too often these days, is it? I suppose you could call it old fashioned. There was a time when people simply said "I'm weary." Sometimes due to physical tiredness, sometimes, when they really weren't sure what was wrong with them, they just knew they had had enough. Now we use new words like depressed, exhausted or stressed, and rush for a tablet to cure all our ills.

Don't get me wrong these are genuine things and the doctor's is a good place to go, no doubt about it. However In *Matthew Chapter: 11 verses 28 – 30,* Jesus has this to say,

*"Come to me, all you who are weary and burdened, and I will give you rest. Take my yoke upon you and learn from me, for I am gentle and humble in heart, and you will find rest for your souls. For my yoke is easy and my burden is light"*

I remember we were once in Malaysia and we were sight-seeing when we came across something I had never seen before. Two oxen yoked together ploughing. As I looked, I saw how impossible it was for one ox to walk at a different pace from the other. There seemed also to be an older ox teamed with a younger one obviously teaching as they walked and worked together.

Allow yourself to be 'yoked' with Jesus, your guide and teacher. He will make light the way because He knows where to tread.

Try to sleep now dear Reader,

*Psalm 62 v1*

*My soul finds rest in God alone; my salvation comes from him.*

*He alone is my rock and my salvation; He is my fortress I shall never be shaken.*

Good night and God bless.

## Shadows

*"Yea though I walk through the valley of the shadow of death I will fear no evil"*

Many, many people are familiar with **verse 4** from **Psalm 23**. Note the writer says "Shadow of death" and not death itself, only its shadow, not the real thing. Shadows cannot in themselves hurt or touch you. Indeed not all shadows are 'scary' depending where they are coming from. Countless children love Tinkerbell and her shadow from the story of Peter Pan. I remember well my brother and I when we were little, my dad would put his two big hands together and with a lamp behind him, cast on the wall the shadow of a rabbit. We loved the rabbit that appeared on the bedroom wall, its ears wiggled, its nose twitched and its two front paws would make it appear to run. Sounds silly now when I think about it but dad and the rabbit told us many a bedtime story and there was no fear just love and a fun time.

**Psalm 17 Verse 8** says **that God will hide you in the shadow of his wings.**

Think about this for a minute, dear Reader as you lie looking at your bedroom wall. Imagine God standing with a great light behind Him and He opens wide His arms and you come to Him and stand so close with your back pressing against His heart then look forward at the shadow cast in front of you. All you would see would be His shadow and your tiny frame would be hidden in Him. There would be no fear or anxiety in you because you would be safe, warm and protected. Stay that close to Him at all times, believe in Him, trust in Him and nothing and no one can harm you.

He loves you now and evermore.

Don't fear the shadows. Good Night, God Bless

# Trust

Why am I awake, Lord? All around me is still and quiet. The air seems a little chilly tonight, perhaps the weather is changing.

"Oh! Hi Reader, good to know I have company. Are you feeling a little uncertain, worrying over something?" You know you should trust God, you know you want to trust him but somehow it is so hard to actually do. Easy to say but at 3 o'clock in the morning, not so easy to do would you agree. Tired, troubled, thinking oh you can do all that, but letting go and trusting well that's a different matter. Why? Why should it be? You know Jesus loves you, He cares for you, His word tells you He will never leave you so what's the problem?

The hymn writer tells us to,

*"Trust and obey for there's no other way, to be happy in Jesus but to trust and obey"*

We have to not only talk the talk but to walk the walk. Every day, every night learn to put your trust in Him who will never let you down.

"But I've been let down so badly in the past!"

"People do, so often they promise and then don't do it"

"We let people down"

Trust me, I'll do it and they never do something happens and they just forget. We feel let down and abandoned in our hour of need. So many of the Psalms speak of trust. Trust in God, his love, his mercy, and His strength.

*Psalm 13 v 5:*

*"But I trust in Your unfailing love"*

# 3 O' CLOCK IN THE MORNING

*Psalm 31 v 14:*

*But I trust in You O Lord.*

On and on verses telling you to trust in Him, His word, His deliverance.

*John 14 v 1* Jesus says,

*"Do not let your hearts be troubled, trust in God, trust also in me"*

This verse is the answer to those troubled thoughts racing through your head. Trust him with them, leave them with him. He's got it all in hand. He won't let you down, that's a promise.

*Hebrews 13 v 5*

*"Never will I leave you; never will I forsake you"*

Try to sleep now Reader, maybe you can't see the way forward but trust him he can.

Good night
God Bless
Love, Beryl

# Understanding

When I first became a Christian, I remember I spent a great deal of time in the Old Testament book, Ecclesiastes. I know it isn't the usual place to start but for some reason that was where the Holy Spirit led me. I believe now it was because I had the desire to try to understand everything I was reading. You see my head knowledge always ruled my heart actions regarding whether or not I could believe in what I was reading. Hope that makes sense to you, Reader! It all had to make sense to me.

To be perfectly honest, in the past whenever I had begun to try to read the Bible and read how old people were, you know Adam lived 930 years, Seth 912, Enosh 815 and so on until Methuselah who lived to 969 years. (You would need a big birthday cake for all those candles) and so because of disbelief and lack of understanding I simply stopped reading. It didn't seem logical, so I lost interest. Only years later when I finally came face to face with the reality of Jesus did I go from head knowledge to heart knowledge and in that moment I knew that I knew, and it all came together. I believed, I understood I knew the truth.

Then when I read the Bible with new insight, new eyes as it were there was this willingness and eagerness to understand. Ask in prayer for the Holy Spirit to reveal his truth, open the Bible and read it, chapter by chapter in a new light and begin to find the wisdom, the understanding and the pearls of His love.

*Ecclesiastes Chapter 3* so beautifully points out that there is a time for everything and a season for every activity under heaven. Solomon shows in these verses the wisdom of doing the right thing at the right time. Sometimes it is good to cry and sometimes there is a time to laugh. Like now, dear Reader, there is a time to be awake and soon there will be a time to sleep. Maybe tonight was God's time for you to be awake to understand more of his word, to get some understanding for your life or it could be that tonight was just the right time to spend time with Him getting to know Him more. Perhaps you can now go to sleep resting in Him in the comfort of knowing Him for who He is and not for just what He can do for you. Making sense of who He is and who you are and why you are where you are right now.

***Proverbs 3 v 5:6***

***Trust in the Lord with all your heart and lean not on your own understanding;***

***In all your ways acknowledge him,***

***and he will make your paths straight.***

Sleep well dear Reader.
Love and kisses.

# Valleys

Do you feel like you are in a valley, dear Reader?

Have you had a high mountain top experience perhaps and now you have plunged into the deep valley? Shadows sweep across the valley blotting out the sun. Sudden coldness, there's fear in the valley. Does the valley seem long and narrow?

*A Psalm of David. Psalm 23 v:4*

*Even though I walk through the valley of the shadow of death,*
*I will fear no evil, for you are with me;*
*your rod and your staff they comfort me.*

David knew all about valleys. He fought the giant Goliath in the Valley of Elah.

*(1 Samuel Chapter 17)*

There are lots more 'valleys' in the Bible. The Valley of Tears, The Valley of Decision,

*Joel 3:14* says "multitudes, multitudes in the valley of decision! The Valley of Dry Bones to name but a few.

*Ezekiel Ch. 37 v1 –14*. This tells how the Lord took Ezekiel to the middle of a valley full of dry bones and he walked up and down amongst them, dry dead bones and...,

Oh! you really must get your Bible out and read this for yourself Reader. You will see how the prophet was to speak to those dry bones, and to tell them about God and how they came to life. Our lives can become very dry when all we do is seemingly walk endlessly on the valley floor. When all hope is gone, we loose heart and lay on the floor and there is no life in us. Is that you right now? Laying down, feeling hopeless, nothing holding you together, or up, no breath in you. Oh, how I hope not.

All is not lost dear Reader. Jesus can and will breathe new life in you. Hear about Jesus, let Him speak to the dryness in your bones Reader, get new life surging through your body, feel alive, renewed. Let Him put His Holy Spirit in you so that you may live.

Remember valleys are places to walk through! My Pastor says "don't pitch your tent in the valley but keep walking through." Maybe, just maybe, the valley is the place where we spend most of our life, learning how to walk and keep walking steadily through life. A place, where we learn to stand up for ourselves and to kill the giants who are trying to defeat us. Keep on keeping on and remember to keep looking up.

*Isaiah 40 v 4*

*Every valley shall be raised up,*
*every mountain and hill made low;*
*the rough ground shall become level,*
*the rugged places plain.*

Good night and God bless.

# Walking On Water

When you're in bed and it is 3 o'clock in the morning you would hardly expect to be thinking about 'Walking on water' now would you? But that is exactly what we are going to do. I know you didn't expect this but life is full of the unexpected and I am hoping that this will challenge you and when tomorrow comes you will consider getting out of your 'comfort boat' and giving it a go.

First the story. We are going to be in *Matthew 14 verses 22 -36* tonight.

Jesus tells his disciples to go on ahead of him and he goes off to pray. They get in their boat and set sail. Suddenly a storm blows up and it gets quite scary even for them. Then around the fourth watch of the night Jesus goes out to them actually walking on the water. Wow! How weird is that? The disciples are understandably terrified thinking they are seeing a ghost BUT he immediately says,

*"It is I, don't be afraid."* Peter answers *"Lord if it is you tell me to come to you on the water."*

*"Come"* he said.

Peter climbs out of the boat over the side onto the rough sea and begins to walk towards Jesus looking at him but then he sees the wind, he becomes afraid and starts to sink. Jesus catches him and rebukes him for his lack of faith. Then they both climb back into the boat together. Obviously I have rushed through this and it is strictly my own version but I know you will want to read through the passage slowly for yourself. Anyway, let us now go back to the beginning and try to 'unpack' as it were, this story together.

What's your boat, dear friend? The place you are most familiar with, where you feel secure, your comfort zone, your home, your office or even your car, perhaps. Trials and tribulations are always coming up, that's life. Things happen suddenly to rock your boat. Sometimes more violently than others, quite unexpectedly things can get very rough. You find yourself hanging onto the sides of your boat; you feel you are drowning and fear sets in. Could be the pile of paperwork facing you, the phone call you have to make tomorrow or even the mountain of ironing facing you. Whatever it is, it seems to be getting bigger and bigger and threatens to sink your boat and you with it.

It's dark, it's getting very rough and it's the fourth watch of the night (my study Bible tells me that is around 3 o'clock in the morning – that's amazing, don't you think? I know I do!)

Why is this the time when things always seem to be at their worst? The boat rocks, the wind howls, it's dark and circumstances just couldn't get any worse, this has to be as bad as it gets and then.................

You see Him. Could this be? Am I seeing things? Could this be Jesus walking through the storm actually on water to come to me? Me, wretched me.

He speaks, *"Take courage! It is I. Don't be afraid."*

Doubt fills Peter (and Reader too!) "Lord, if it's you," Peter replied, "tell me to come to you on the water."

*Verse 29 "Come,"* he said.

Peter gets out of the boat and walks on the water but when he sees the wind he becomes afraid and begins to sink. He cries out "Lord save me" Have you tried getting out of the boat once but the storm was too fierce. Maybe you didn't know Jesus then, you sank and things got worse. Now you are remembering that time and you are afraid. Look what Jesus did. Immediately, yes, immediately Jesus reached out his hand and caught him.

Cry out to him and he will save you. Oh yes, he may say "You of little faith, why did you doubt?" but look at *verse 32*. And when they climbed (note: they climbed) into the boat, the wind died down.

When Jesus is in the situation with you the wind calms down. You are not on your own.

Dear Reader, it is a huge step the step of faith but He is there for you and with you. You are not on your own. I hope the wind and waves are calming down for you right now.

Rest Jesus is in the boat with you.

Peace be still.

God Bless.

## Xerxes

I've put King Xerxes in this little book because in *Esther Chapter 6 v 1*, it says:

*'That night the king could not sleep; so he ordered the book of the chronicles, the record of his reign, to be brought in and read to him.'*

Even kings cannot sleep sometimes, so you are in good company. However this king did what I suggested in my comments with which I introduced this little book – he did something useful with his time while he was awake, he read, or rather he had his attendant read to him (I expect his book was a lot bigger than ours) and by this, he discovered some pretty useful information. You can find the whole story of King Xerxes in the Book of Esther in the Old Testament.

As a quick overview, (my version you must understand).

King Xerxes was a very powerful and wealthy Persian king who ruled round 486-465 BC. He deposed his wife Queen Vashti after she refused his command to come to a banquet he was giving and he later married Esther. Actually, I do think you would be wise to read this fascinating short book of only 10 chapters' for yourself, as I know you will thoroughly enjoy it.

A powerful king, much feasting and wine being drunk, two beautiful women, a plot, a hanging, tension, intrigue and bravery. Wow! all in all by today's standard a 'best seller' and Esther's famous line ending in *Chapter 4: 16*

*"And if I perish, I perish."*

This brave young woman's courage to speak up, putting her own life at risk to save her people, the Jews.

"Lord when we lie awake and we read Your word, help us by Your

Holy Spirit to be guided to the things that can change our thinking and bring us closer to you. To know you more, to understand your ways and to know your heart."

Please read *Psalm 143* and *v 8 –10* especially.

*Let the morning bring me word of your unfailing love,*
*For I have put my trust in you.*
*Show me the way I should go,*
*For to you I lift up my soul.*
*Rescue me from my enemies, O Lord,*
*For I hide myself in you.*
*Teach me to do your will,*
*For you are my God; may your good Spirit lead me on level ground.*

Good night, dear Reader you may not feel much like a king tonight but according to …

*Galatians 3 verse 29,* which says,

*"If you belong to Christ, then you are Abraham's seed, and heirs according to the promise."*

Now you really have to sleep better knowing that don't you agree?
Good night and sleep well.

# 3 O' CLOCK IN THE MORNING

## Yesterday Has Gone

Maybe you are thinking this is a strange heading but I have a feeling that tonight, dear Reader you can cope with something quite different.

Are you ready?

I want you to try to imagine yourself as an Israelite slave in Egypt in about BC 1446. Life is extremely hard. Maybe you have to make bricks day after day after day, or perhaps you are the one to collect the straw  or the clay to make them with.  It is hot and dirty work. You get fed, yes that's true but it is barely enough and there is no choice. Maybe you make clothes, cook, wash, clean, whatever you do it is day after day after day. You are kicked, beaten, ill-treated, get no thanks, no holidays, no rest from your hard labour. Work, eat, work, sleep, day after day after day. Then along comes Moses and your life changes.

Please read the story in *Exodus 12: v 31* onwards.

Eventually after so many amazing things have happened the children of Israel find themselves free, their own masters after about 400 years of slavery. They are on the way to the land their forefather's told them about - The Promised Land, a land flowing with milk and honey. Wow!

Mind you, they are for now wandering around in a desert in what they stand up in and the Promised Land seems to be a good fair way off as yet. Still, they are free!

However being human what do you think they do? Yes, you're right, they start grumbling. Oh! Not you, I know you wouldn't grumble, dear Reader, or would you?

Suddenly, their yesterdays looked so much better than their todays and they couldn't see their tomorrows. They just looked back and saw only the good things or what they wanted to remember. How many people do you hear today doing that constantly?

"When I was nowt but a lad we used to only have bread and jam but it was reet good"

Well, was it? Maybe it was but if you were to offer the same today for their tea I think their face would show a different picture. Some people live on their yesterdays and sacrifice their todays. Always looking back or re-telling the same stories but adding little 'bits' all the time. The sky wasn't always blue, summers weren't always hot, it rained and we had fog. Life went on, but it was just different.

Some of yesterday's happenings were wonderful, please don't misunderstand me and we can look back with fond and happy memories, some we need to deal with, forget, get over and move on. Remember that today will soon be tomorrow's yesterday so all the more reason to make today as good as we can. Look forward, move forward and follow the Good Shepherd. Let Him lead and guide, then all our today's will fill our yesterdays with lasting happy memories and our tomorrows with expectant hope.

You are not a slave to sin and death, dear Reader, you have been bought with the precious blood of Christ. You are free.

Good night dear Reader,

God Bless you.
Love, Beryl

## Zephaniah

Well, here we are Reader, can you believe how far we have come? We have steadily worked through so many topics together, climbed a good few mountains and walked through some valleys. The Lord has been our guide and shepherd and I have so valued your friendship on this journey together, and here we are at the final letter 'Z'.

Actually, I now feel there are so many other subjects we could and should share together, I almost feel we have only scratched the surface. When you get to know someone, it gets easier to talk on a deeper level, don't you agree? That is how I hope you now feel towards Jesus.

Talk to him, thank him, praise him and most importantly pray. God really does answer prayer. Our God is a great God and never forget that He loves you. You are special.

The prophet *Zephaniah in Chapter 3 verse 20* writes:

*"At that time I will gather you;*
*At that time I will bring you home.*
*I will give you honour and praise*
*among all the peoples of the earth*
*when I restore your fortunes*
*before your very eyes."*
*Says the Lord.*

Good night dear Reader, my friend.

Sleep well and God Bless you.

With love from
Beryl

## We've Done it, Reader

Yes we've done it, Reader. Between the three of us, we've written our 'little book'.

God inspired me, I've talked and studied with Him, I've talked and studied with you, we've listened to each other, you've read and oh how I so hope you have listened to what He has said to you, inspired you and comforted you. These 3 o'clock in a morning times have been so special. Praying together, crying together and learning together. You have become very special to me, dear Reader. Life goes on and we all have our special times. Needs come and go and seasons change. Learn to cope with change, be ready for the many changes life presents to you.

As you grow in your new found faith and years dear Reader I pray that your nights will be filled with peace and your days with joy. Walk with God, pray with Him and to Him, remember to trust in Him. Sow good seeds that will bring many good harvests into your life. Be strong in Him; He won't let you down.

When next you wake at 3 o'clock in the morning, make it a time to pray and give thanks for His love, His goodness and His mercy.

*Psalm 4 verse 8*

*I will lie down and sleep in peace,*
*for you alone, O Lord, make me dwell in safety.*

It has been such a pleasure meeting you, my friend. Maybe this is the end of our 'Little Book' together but I hope and pray that for you, Reader, it is just the beginning.

Good night and God Bless.
Sleep well.
All my love, Beryl

## A letter from Beryl's brother

Dear Sister-Woman,
3 a.m. is a time when I am normally asleep, yet as I read this book I am conscious of a deep affinity with it's circumstances. 3 a.m. reminds me of the time when we read in the Bible that Peter in the middle of a storm did the impossible because of Jesus. **(Mt.14 v 24-33)**

This little book tells me of 3 a.m. times through which you, my little sister have been enabled to do something special for each of us. The ones who are often awake at 3 a.m. meet in your little book a companion who understands and who can share the grace and contentment you have received in Christ. The ones who normally sleep at 3 a.m. receive in your little book a map,a compass and a guide to prepare them for their "3 a.m. times" whenever they may come. The ones who find they are called to share with those going through "3 a.m. times" find in your little book an easy reference to difficult and personal issues. Thank you for being obedient . Thank you for your faith. Thank you for this book.

Thank you Beryl. As a child you always had the first of any illness which meant that I although older, was protected or prepared. Thank you Beryl for your "3 a.m. times" also protect and prepare me and I feel sure all who read your book.

Thank you sister for you have shared your heart and experience in ways that richly encourage us all. May you be blessed by the discovery of many new brothers and sisters in Christ through this wonderful little book.

With love and thanks
David

Beryl's next book is called: **Follow the Cloud**

This book deals with the circumstances of life
that consume our days. During the night we can long for the day,
but the day can present a whole new set of problems and
up's and down's for us to deal with.

Beryl discusses everyday subjects such as retail therapy,
instant coffee, moving house and even finding and losing your
keys. Fun things, difficult things and sad things but with Jesus,
Beryl and you Reader things won't seem half so bad.

*Beryl's Little Books*
www.berylslittlebooks.co.uk
(see my range of complementary
gifts)
email: info@berylslittlebooks.co.uk
Tel: 01524 401940
Fax: 01524 831939      281

# 3 O' CLOCK IN THE MORNING

Dear Reader,

We have come so far together the three of us and now you are ready. Use these pages as your own little book. Make notes, draw pictures, write the letter you know you should have done so long ago, write to Jesus, anything but just do it.

_____

_____

_____

_____

_____

_____

_____

_____

_____

_____

_____

_____

# 3 O' CLOCK IN THE MORNING

# 3 O' CLOCK IN THE MORNING

# 3 O' CLOCK IN THE MORNING

# 3 O' CLOCK IN THE MORNING

# 3 O' CLOCK IN THE MORNING

# 3 O' CLOCK IN THE MORNING

## 3 O' CLOCK IN THE MORNING

## 3 O' CLOCK IN THE MORNING

## 3 O' CLOCK IN THE MORNING

# 3 O' CLOCK IN THE MORNING